See God With Open Eyes

SUKHDEV VIRDEE

Copyright © 2019 Sukhdev Virdee

All rights reserved.

ISBN: 9781794661813

DEDICATION

Dedicated to the Absolute Divine
Truth That **YOU** Are!

Whole heartedly dedicated to
Lord Krishna, Lord Shiva,
Sri Ramana Maharshi and
Guru Nanak Dev Ji who have been and are
My Spiritual Guides on the path to
Self Realization and God Realization.

CONTENTS

	Acknowledgments	i
1	The Story Before The Story	1
2	The Story	7
3	Brahman: The Absolute Reality	17
4	Knowledge	33
5	Truth	51
6	Guruji in Mussorrie	67
7	Mussorrie to Vatsalya	85
8	After the Story	91
9	Extra Notes	95
10	About The Author	103

ACKNOWLEDGMENTS

There are three friends that I have to absolutely acknowledge who knowingly or unknowingly led me to realize the Absolute Truth.

The first is Vik Sharma, the most hyperactive friend I have. He introduced me to Lord Krishna.

The second friend is Rajeev Aryan, an awakened being himself. He introduced me to the Bhagavad Gita and predicted that I would soon have a similar awakening.
This led to Self-Realization through complete surrender, love and devotion.

The third friend is Ranjan Sahu, a living encyclopedia of Spiritual Scriptures. He was sent by Lord Krishna to guide me on the path of knowledge, the Highest Truth.
This led to God-Realization through direct experiential knowledge.

THE STORY BEFORE THE STORY

We all have asked this question in our childhood, *"Mom where is God?"* And the answer usually came immediately, *"My child, God is everywhere."* And the child probes further, *"Mom, if God is everywhere then why can't I see Him?"* And the mother replies, *"You can't see God because He is all-powerful and can do anything He likes. If you believe in Him and love Him sincerely with all your heart, He will show Himself to you one day. Pray to Him my child."*

The conversation stops right there and the child grows up praying occasionally and doing all the normal activities that children do and after a few years he or she soon finds himself or herself completely involved in life, building a career, building and maintaining relationships, learning new things at school, going through good times and unpleasant times, looking forward to creating a stable future for himself or herself. A tiny part may still linger around yearning to know God, but life presents enough distractions for one to become *serious* about life itself. A person who has acquired lots of wealth, one who becomes famous, one who is the best at the work they do and so on become the *"measurement"* for a successful life.

Life offers great luxuries, pleasures and experiences and if one wants to acquire them then one needs to work hard and earn lots of money with which one can '*buy*' this so called '*happiness*'.

So, name, fame and fortune become the primary goal of life and God takes a backseat. Everyone wants to become a millionaire. The millionaire wants to become a billionaire, the billionaire wants to become a multi-billionaire, the multi-billionaire is striving to become the world's richest person and the world's richest person is striving to retain the number one position.

There is no end to the human desires. It is not wrong to pursue one's desires but only the wise person will realize that every happiness that this world and life has to offer is temporary. In fact there is nothing in the Universe that isn't subject to change and change is the only constant in life.

At this point the common man says, *"I know everything is temporary, things can give happiness for a little while, relationships can give happiness too, money can buy luxuries and comforts and everything will end for me when I die. I know that I will die someday but that should not stop me from having or acquiring a good comfortable life while I am still alive in this world."*

And thus the common man accepts life with all its ups and downs, hardships and is constantly in search of happiness and trying to avoid pain and sorrow. This has become the goal of life and the very definition of the word 'success'. *"The wealthier you are, the more successful you are and the happier you are,"* is the most common misconception that we have today and almost everyone is striving to achieve that in some way or another.

Back to the child who asked, *"Why can't I see God if He is everywhere?"* I ask you to bring that child back into your mind and ask this question again with the same *freshness* that you had in your childhood because the answer given (by the revealed scriptures) in the story ahead will remarkably take that question head-on and answer it beyond any doubt whatsoever. You will undoubtedly begin to recognize the Supreme Being everywhere, every time and in everything around you and realize how you've been missing Him/Her/It a thousand times in every moment of your life.

This book is based upon only one verse from the oldest Holy Scriptures known to mankind, the *Vedas. (Taittiriya Upanishad, Part 2: Bliss of Brahman. Chapter 1 Verse 3 "Om. He who knows Brahman attains the Highest. On the above, the following mantra is recorded:* **"He who knows Brahman which is Truth, Knowledge and Infinity,** *hidden in the cave of the heart and in the highest akasa-he, being one with the omniscient Brahman, enjoys simultaneously all desires.")*

This verse is from the 'Taittiriya Upanishad' (found in the Yajurveda) which when translated from the original Sanskrit to English defines the Ultimate Reality of the Universe, the Supreme Being, 'Brahman' as 'Truth, Knowledge and Infinity!'

In the coming pages the definition is explained in very simple words that have been woven inside a beautiful little story with fictional characters that conveys the true ancient teachings of the Upanishad. By the end of this little book *(it is purposely kept to just over a hundred pages)* you, the reader should and will be able to see the Supreme Being everywhere without a doubt and without having to resort to blind faith or belief.

*See God
With
Open Eyes*

SEE GOD WITH OPEN EYES

THE STORY

David was excited as the pilot announced their descent towards the Indira Gandhi International Airport in New Delhi. It had been a long flight from New York City, fourteen hours to be exact, yet David's eyes beamed with excitement and he couldn't get rid of the grin on his face. He was at the peak of his medical career in the Big Apple, working over sixty hours a week in various hospitals where he was called upon for surgery. He was a heart transplant specialist who had performed over two hundred heart transplant surgeries of which none had gone wrong till date. He was a much sought after heart surgeon among all the hospitals in New York.

At the peak of his successful career, he took an indefinite break to come on this trip that he believed would change his life. He had finally gotten permission after a wait of over two years, to visit the great sage popularly known as Swamiji. He had posted a letter to the ashram two years back and had waited since then to get a reply allowing him to come and stay a few days at the ashram and spend some personal time with Swamiji himself. This was an opportunity that he wouldn't have let go even if it meant he lost all his name, fame and fortune. He knew how life transforming a meeting with Swamiji could be.

As he stepped out of the airport with just a small backpack containing only his very basic essentials, he looked around for the local guide he had hired for the trip. Uchit was a young boy from the Himalayas who now lived in New Delhi and was earning a living by guiding tourists around the city. He had a mobile phone and was also active on social media, which is how David had gotten in touch with him and hired his services.

David looked around and saw an enthusiastic boy waving frantically at him, Uchit was quite an energetic boy, in his early twenties and David recognized him immediately. Standing next to Uchit, was an older man, wearing a long orange robe with long black curly hair and beads around his neck. He was holding a placard with David's name on it. David thought for a moment, *"could it be?"* he asked himself as he walked towards both of them.

Both men welcomed David with smiles and a hug. Uchit quickly relieved him of his backpack. *"Are you Yogiji from the ashram?"* asked David excitedly. He recalled posting another letter to the ashram requesting if someone could come to receive him at the airport but hadn't received any reply. Yogiji had written the first reply to David confirming his stay at the ashram and David guessed it would be him, as the ashram had very limited staff, mostly volunteers who did the daily chores out of love for Swamiji.

"Yes I am Yogiji from the ashram and we received your letter and request. Swamiji especially asked me to come and receive you from the airport; it's a long journey back to the ashram from here. It's also a 'special mission' for me, as you will find out once we board the train in the morning." It was almost 2am and the train to Dehradun was at 6:50am.

The travel itinerary included a six-hour train journey from New Delhi to Dehradun and then a three-hour taxi ride to Vatsalya Village where the ashram was located. The taxi ride from the airport to the train station took roughly forty-five minutes.

Once at the station Uchit led them to a small *chai* shop just outside the station where they served the best *chai* and hot *samosas* all through the night. It was a popular eating spot, open day and night, and passengers who reached the station early often came there to have a snack before boarding their trains.

"Is it true that Swamiji has seen God and can show us God if he wants?" David asked Yogiji with a childlike excitement in his eyes. This is what David had come for. Since his childhood he had a burning desire within to be able to see God and talk to Him like a friend, ask Him about the creation of the Universe, get His help to accomplish what he desired in life and most importantly also find out the purpose of life and everything else that went on in the Universe.

It seemed like no one had a clue, all the religious places he visited often spoke about God and praised His glories but none could honestly say they could *show* you God or even make you have a *conversation* with Him.

David wanted to see and talk to God one-on-one *if* God existed. He didn't want to spend his life just wondering if God was real. *"There is a Creation so there must be a Creator and I would like to meet my Creator. Is that too much to ask?"* That was what he would ask the religious headmen in temples, churches, synagogues and other religious places he often visited when he was off work.

He was almost giving up the thought of finding anyone who could show him God when one day he saw a post on social media saying, *"God is looking for you. Are you willing to meet Him too?"* It was a post from one of his social media friends, you know, the ones you have never met in person.

He followed up the post and found out it was a popular claim and quote by Swamiji. After a thorough research and reading up about Swamijis disciple's experiences on the Internet, he could not wait to go see the man himself. Vatsalya Village has no Internet and phone facilities and all communications at the ashram were done through the Indian Post Office.

David had searched the Internet for pictures and information of Vatsalya Village. It was a beautiful Himalayan village on the banks of the Ganges River with no telephone networks, no tourist traps and mountains all around. Home to roughly a thousand people and their animals; it was a perfect getaway place for nature lovers. David was looking forward to spending time in the Himalayan Mountains and getting to know the local villagers as well apart from his main mission, seeing God!

"Many have come to Swamiji and by His grace some have been able to see God within a short time. What is your idea of God? What is God like?" Yogiji asked David as the final whistle blew and they boarded the *Shatabdi Express.* David looked impressed with the interiors of the train. He had heard many horrific stories about traveling in India, but this was quite good and decent, promising a smooth ride. After all it was a six-hour train journey to Dehradun.

After settling down on their seats David replied to Yogiji, *"In my opinion and from what I've heard from different people since my childhood is that God is kind, loving, merciful, generous. He listens to our prayers and some people do get what they ask of Him. I'm not sure what He would look like but everyone says He is formless. He lives in Heaven where everything is beautiful and there is no suffering. All good human beings go and live with Him in heaven after they die, and the evil ones go to hell where they are punished for their sins. But sometimes I wonder, if God were really there why would He let all this suffering continue in the world, why would He make innocent children suffer, keep beggars hungry and homeless. There are many such questions that arise when I see the 'not-so-good' events happening in the world. I would definitely ask Him all this if I get to see and talk with Him. Can Swamiji really show me God? I'm burning up inside to meet Him."*

By the time David finished, both Yogiji and Uchit were staring at him, trying to imagine all the things he was saying about God. Just then it struck David and he asked Yogiji in excitement, *"Yogiji, what is your 'special mission' on this trip? You said you would reveal it once we boarded the train."*

Yogiji replied, *"Oh yes! You see, only a few spiritual seekers from the west are personally approved by Swamiji to meet him and you are one of them. Whenever such a seeker arrives, it is my duty to receive and prepare him or her with a little knowledge from our ancient scriptures that talk about Brahman - the Absolute Reality. This is done so that once you are in Swamiji's presence you will already have a firm foundation and understanding of 'when', 'where' and in 'what' 'Brahman' appears before us. You will also not be in shock when Swamiji introduces you to God as you will already know 'Brahman'."*

"Brahman? Who...or should I ask 'what' is Brahman?" asked David with a puzzled look on his face. *"Okay, here we go, I'll try to cover as much as I can before we get to Vatsalya Village. We do have enough time on our hands but I'll still try and make it as simple, clear and easy to understand as I possibly can. Just a while ago you said that everyone says they haven't seen God because He is 'formless'."*

"Yes," replied David *"Well 'Brahman – the Absolute Reality' is the One Formless Universal Supreme Being on which the entire Universe rests. 'Brahman' is 'God' without any qualities or attributes. 'Brahman' is indescribable; language cannot express what this Supreme Being is, yet It is every-where, every-time and in every-thing! And it is my duty to show you this Absolute Reality called Brahman before we get to the ashram."*

Both David and Uchit looked astonished, their eyes wide open and jaws almost touching the floor.

"Please repeat that again." David could not believe what he had just heard. *"Well, 'Brahman' is the One Formless Supreme..."* *"No, no, I heard that part, what did you say after that?"* David's voice was quivering. *"Umm.. That it is my duty to show you Brahman before we get to the ashram?"* replied Yogiji softly with a surprised look in his eyes, begging for a confirmation of what he had just said.

"Really? You mean it? You really really like REALLY mean it? Just a minute!" shouted David in disbelief, *"Quick! Uchachit get my bag!"* cried out David looking at Uchit. *"Sir my name is not Uchachit, it's Uchit, and it means 'correct',"* replied Uchit standing up to reach the bag before handing it over to David. *"I'm so sorry Uchit, I'm really excited, and I want you to jot down ALL the important points from Yogijis talk just in case I forget them,"* said David while handing him a notebook and a marker from his bag.

"And 'Uchit' you said means 'correct'? Is that correct? Am I uchit?" he said jokingly. Uchit gave him a stern look, snatched the notebook and marker and wrote down the following on the first page...

The Word Used In The Ancient Scriptures Of The East Referring To The Supreme Being Is 'Brahman'.

BRAHMAN:
THE ABSOLUTE REALITY

Yogiji carried on, *"Our ancient scriptures say that 'Brahman' is the ever-unchanging, permanent highest reality. When you say God is kind, merciful, loving, great, generous and so on, these are all different qualities or attributes of God. 'Brahman' is formless and has no qualities or attributes. One cannot say Brahman is anything like loving, kind, generous or merciful. No, Brahman simply IS! If you understand just the 'definition' of Brahman, you'll be well on your way to being an enlightened soul."*

David nodded his head and Yogiji started, *"The 'Taittiriya Upanishad' (that is found in the Yajurveda) defines Brahman as 'Truth-Knowledge-Infinity' simultaneously. This means that Brahman is Infinite Truth and Infinite*

Knowledge, not truth at one time, knowledge at another and infinity at another. No, Brahman is all three together at once! Only when you see or perceive all three 'together' will you see and understand the formless Supreme Being - Brahman.

And to understand this definition in it's complete and true sense I'll start from the last word, 'infinity' and work backwards. By the time we reach the ashram, you will not only have understood Brahman but you will see Brahman EVERY-WHERE, EVERY-TIME and in EVERY-THING, this much I can promise you!" David and Uchit were all ears sitting at the edge of their seats, facing Yogiji and looking directly into his eyes.

"Infinity means without limit, without boundaries, impossible to measure or calculate. According to the ancient teachings there are three types of limitations in the Universe. Everything we see and perceive is limited in SPACE, TIME and OBJECT IDENTITY. This means that everything we see or know is not infinite, not permanent and keeps changing within these three limitations. Let's take a deeper look at each of these limitations."

"SPACE limitation means that something is occupying a certain amount of space and not the rest of the space around it. It is taking up only a certain amount of space, so there is a certain point where it begins to occupy Space and then there's an ending point where it stops occupying Space. In simple words everything you see is somewhere, not everywhere."

"For example, the seat that you are sitting on is here and not there, nor is it anywhere else in the universe. The words 'where, here' and 'there' denote space. In the same way everything you can see is precisely where it is and not anywhere else.

Your body is occupying only a certain amount of space in this train. Your bag is up there on the stand and not here. Everything we know has a limitation in space."

"Even the largest countries have borders, the largest continent has seashores, the highest mountain has a peak, the deepest ocean has a seabed. The Earth occupies only a tiny amount of space in the Universe and even our galaxy the 'Milky Way' doesn't occupy the entire Universe. Everything has a starting point in space and an ending point in space. Everything is limited in space! Take a moment to think about it."

David scratched his head and thought, making hilarious expressions while thinking before finally nodding in agreement. *"You're right Yogiji, there is nothing I can think of that is everywhere except space itself, please continue."*

Yogiji had a smile on his face. He knew the scriptures are never wrong but loved to see someone attempt to question them to clear their doubts.

He continued, *"Now imagine if there is something that has no limitation in Space. No limitation in Space would mean that there is nowhere in the Universe that it is not. It is equally present every-where at the same time. It is here, there and everywhere simultaneously. If there were such a thing, it would be called "Omnipresent."*

"Omnipresent means 'present in all places at all times'. The Upanishad says that Brahman is infinity; therefore Brahman is not limited in Space, which means that BRAHMAN IS OMNIPRESENT!"

"There is no space in the Universe where Brahman is not!" Yogiji stopped to see whether David was following. David looked at Uchit, *"I hope you're noting the important points dude?"* Uchit showed him the page where he had scribbled...

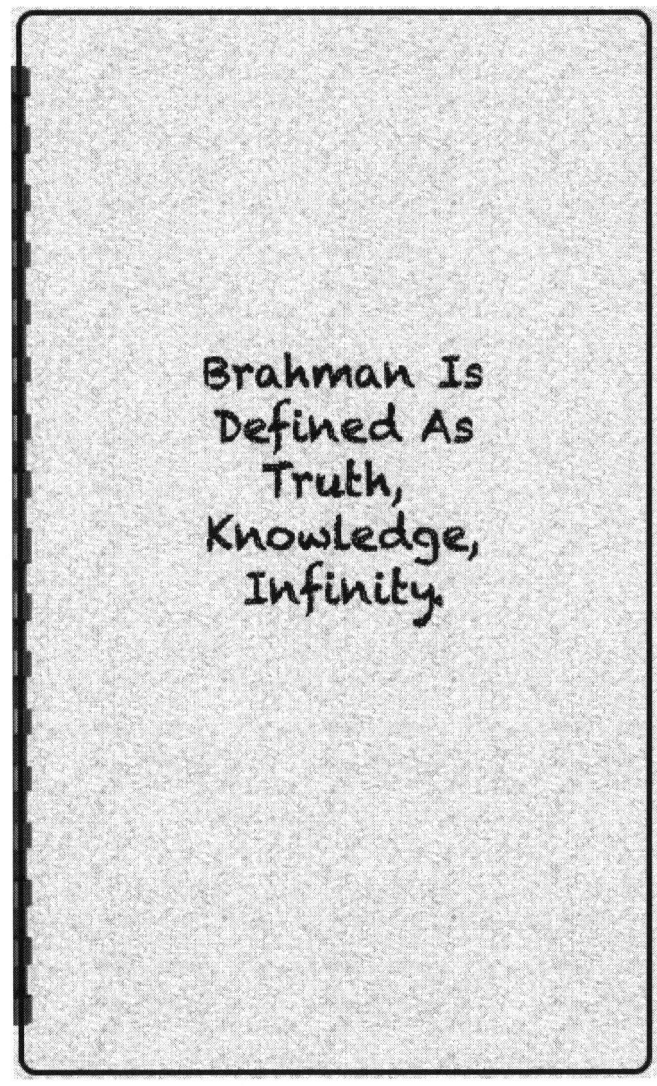

Pleased with Uchit's understanding Yogiji continued, *"TIME is mentioned as the second limitation. Time limitation means that something has a point in time when it comes into existence and a point in time when it goes out of existence. In between these two points in time the object 'exists'. Everything we can see around us or even perceive with our minds is limited in time. For example, the marker Uchit is taking notes with. There was a time when it was created and now it exists and there will come a time when it will be destroyed. People are born and they die, things are created and later are destroyed. This train was created and will in the future be destroyed."*

"Everything in nature changes with time as well. The trees and vegetation you see outside will grow with time and dry up soon. The hills and mountains keep eroding and volcanoes erupt again, the landscape is never constant. Everything is subject to change in time. The Universe as we know it, is temporary and nothing remains the same forever. David can you think of something that doesn't have a beginning or doesn't change with time?" This time David was quick to answer in the negative. *"Nope! Nothing remains the same forever. I know that."*

"Now, imagine if there is something that didn't have this limitation? That would mean that there is no point in time when it came into existence and there is no point in time when it would go out of existence. An easier way of saying the same thing is that 'it was, is and will always be'. So, if there were anything like this in the Universe it would be called "eternal" or "timeless".

"Since Brahman is infinite and not limited in any way, BRAHMAN IS ETERNAL OR TIMELESS! There is no time in the Universe when Brahman is not! I think you get that; it's not very difficult to grasp. So far we now know that Brahman is omnipresent and eternal. Are you still with me David? Please ask any questions that may arise in your mind.

The Scriptures urge you to ask questions and clear any doubts you may have. Since your childhood you may have been accustomed to 'believing' or having 'blind faith' that God exists without questioning His existence, we don't encourage that. Please ask and clear any doubts that arise as we go along." David nodded, *"Sure I will. And the third limitation is Object Identity right?"*

Yogiji smiled, *"Yes. OBJECT IDENTITY limitation means that an object is limited to 'what it is' and not any other object. For example, this train ticket is this particular ticket and not the seat, not the window, not the trees outside. It is limited to being only this particular ticket and not anything else. Your passport denotes that you are David and not any other identity in the world. You are limited to being you and not any other thing, person or object."*

"Everything we see or perceive has this limitation. This kind of limitation should be simple to understand; this marker is not the notebook, this train is not the trees, the window is not the door, New York is not New Delhi and so on and so forth. Take a look around and check it out for yourself," said Yogiji confidently. *"Nope! No need to do that. Every object is different from another, that's common sense. Please carry on,"* replied David.

"Again, now, imagine if there is something that doesn't have this object limitation? It would mean that it is not limited to any one object. Alternatively we can say that there is no object in the Universe that is not it. If there is no other 'thing' or 'object' that it is 'not', then it means that there is only 'one' thing or 'one' object in the entire Universe. Every-thing is ONE! According to the ancient scriptures this is referred to as 'non-dual' which means 'not two' or no second thing apart from it."

"Therefore according to the definition, BRAHMAN IS NON-DUAL. (No second thing or object exists apart from Brahman). There is no object (physical or non-physical) in the Universe that Brahman is not! We have now discovered that Brahman is Omnipresent, Eternal and Non-Dual." David sat still, shaking his head in amazement, *"You got all that from the one word 'infinity'? I've never thought about infinity in this way. This is absolutely fascinating! And surprise surprise! There's nothing that I can question or disagree with. It's all sounds very logical and makes sense so far."*

At that moment the ticket collector walked into the coach and announced for everyone to keep their tickets ready for inspection. Uchit was already waving his hand holding their three tickets as if he had been waiting for the collector to walk in. The ticket collector promptly checked the tickets, smiled at Yogiji and asked in Hindi, *"Kya sikha rahe ho aaj Yogiji? (What are you teaching today Yogiji?).* Yogiji replied *"America se aaye hai, inko Brahman samjhana hai ashram ponch ne se pehele."* (He has come from America and I have to teach him about Brahman before we reach the ashram).

The ticket collector looked at David, shook his head in disbelief and said, *"Ye wala nahi samaj payega Yogiji, wapas bhejdo isse, Swamiji kahi naraz na hojaye." (He doesn't look the type who will understand Yogiji, send him back before Swamiji gets annoyed).* Everyone in the coach burst out laughing including Uchit. One angry look from David and Uchit quickly grabbed the notebook, composed himself and wrote down the following on a new page...

'Brahman' Is Everywhere, Every time in Everything!

Therefore 'Brahman' Is Omnipresent, Eternal & Non-Dual!

The train slowed down and after about 2 minutes pulled into Muzaffarnagar Station. The train would halt for ten minutes and that was enough time to get down for a snack and some *chai*. As the three got off the train one could hear the hustle and bustle of people getting on and off the coaches, *coolies* rushing into the train compartments carrying out luggage on their heads. The hawkers also walked into the train selling all sorts of snacks and soft drinks. It was a very busy station and all the vendors seemed to be making the most of the ten-minute halt.

Uchit led them to one of the *chai* stalls on the platform. David watched, as what he thought was a simple train station, looked more like a bustling market place at peak hours. So many people, so much activity going on, people shouting here and there, luggage being off-loaded, more being loaded, the ticket collectors meeting on the platform, children crying, others playing and laughing on the platform, each one trying to get their job done before the train leaves and yet no one seemed to mind the 'organized chaos' that he was witnessing. *"This is incredible!"* he thought. He never had the time to stop and observe what went on at the train platforms in New York. Everyone there is so busy on their mobile phones to notice anything else.

Sipping hot *chai* from a little glass and munching on fried *pakoras* this time, he reflected on what Yogiji had spoken about. Nothing even on this busy train platform was infinite in anyway. *"Everything actually is limited in space, time and object identity."* He thought to himself as he took the last bite of a potato *pakora.* He recalled some familiar sayings he had heard during childhood, *"Everything is subject to change", "Nothing remains the same forever", "The Buddha says everything in the world is not only temporary but momentary".* Now he could comprehend the meaning of all these *cliché* wisdom sayings.

The whistle blew and all three quickly boarded the train. From the window David was stunned to see people still boarding a moving train, the doors remained open even after the train started to move. That would have amounted to high security and safety lapses in New York.

David started off, *"Yogiji, what you have explained and described so far I have no problem understanding, but this Brahman sounds like what most people think and believe God to be like. You have simply replaced the word 'God' with the word 'Brahman'. We have all heard and read about this since childhood that God is every-where, every-time and in every-thing but I still can't see God or even the Brahman that you're talking about anywhere, anytime or in anything!"*

David continued, *"In fact, if Brahman is every-where, every-time and every-thing then you should be able to show me Brahman right here, right now in anything I choose to point to! Is that possible? If not, then you're wasting my time because I came here looking for someone who has seen God and can show me God, not someone who has just simply heard about God."*

Yogiji looked at David with a warm smile and said, *"My dear boy, Brahman is every-where, every-time and every-thing. That is the truth! Just listen and try to understand the definition in it's entirety first. Have some faith that the ancient scriptures are not lying, be patient and I promise you by the time we reach the ashram, you will be seeing Brahman every-where! You will be seeing Brahman every-time! You will be seeing Brahman in every-thing! Again, this is my promise!"* David nodded his head to carry on.

"From the definition you have now understood the word 'infinity'. Let's try and understand the other two words; 'truth' and 'knowledge'. These are words you must be very familiar with and maybe use on almost a daily basis in your worldly life. I'm sure you must have a pretty good idea of what they mean too, but remember, Brahman is all three words (Truth, Knowledge, Infinity) simultaneously! i.e. Truth has to be knowledge and infinity as well to be Brahman. Knowledge has to be truth and infinity as well to be Brahman. Infinity should be truth and knowledge as well to be Brahman.

Truth + Knowledge + Infinity = Brahman. Great, now let's move on to Knowledge."

KNOWLEDGE

Yogiji cleared his throat and continued with regained freshness in his voice, *"Remember we are working our way backwards to understand the definition of Brahman. The most accepted definition of the word knowledge is: Knowledge is a familiarity, awareness or understanding of someone or something such as facts, information, descriptions or skills which is acquired through experience or education by perceiving, discovering or learning."*

"According to the ancient scriptures, for any knowledge that exists there must be 3 entities; the knower, the known and the knowledge itself. For example, I know that this boy is called Uchit. In this case 'I' am the knower, 'this boy' is the known and that 'his name is Uchit' is the knowledge. "I ate samosas!". "I" am the knower, "samosas" is the known and "I ate samosas" is the knowledge. "This is a marker." "I" am the knower

"this object" is the known and the fact that "it is called a marker" is the knowledge. In this way you will find that everything you know is 'knowledge' and that it includes 'you' as the 'knower' and the 'object' as the 'known'." David listened intently while Uchit scribbled something on a new page...

'Knowledge'
Requires
3 Entities:
The Knower,
The Known
And
The Knowledge!

Yogiji carried on, *"Anything that you know is knowledge, but let's see as per the definition whether knowledge is 'truth' and 'infinity' as well."*

"David, how does any knowledge 'exist' in the Universe?" David instantly replied *"It exists in our thoughts, memories, imagination, emotions, dreams, books, magazines, newspapers, radio, television and so on. Apart from this, anything and everything we 'experience' or 'perceive' is also knowledge. Everything in our awareness is knowledge."*

Yogiji questioned, *"Is all the knowledge you just mentioned now, 'true'?"* and before David could open his mouth Yogiji blurted out excitedly, *"Of course it's true! Everything we think, remember, feel, dream, the knowledge in books, magazines, radio and television 'exists!' Even a lie or wrong information 'exists'. Just the fact that there is any kind of knowledge means it 'exists' and therefore must be true! The knowledge may be wrong but the fact that it 'exists' is true."*

"The same applies to any kind of 'experience' as well. It could be an experience in your life, in your imagination, in your dream, your thoughts and so on. The fact that you 'experienced' it, is true!" David thought about it, *"So, all our lives we have one experience after another, all that is knowledge. What we learned in school, college and university is all knowledge. All our thoughts, dreams and imagination are also knowledge. Newspapers, music, scents, sights, and in fact everything we perceive is knowledge. Wow! I never looked at it that way before. I guess*

everything in our minds qualifies as knowledge which does 'exist' making it all 'true.' Is that uchit Yogiji?" "*That indeed is Uchit!*" replied Yogiji looking at Uchit who wasn't finding his name being used to crack jokes funny at all.

"*So we can safely say that ALL KNOWLEDGE IS TRUE! It doesn't mean that what the knowledge is saying is true; just the fact that the knowledge 'exists' is true. Now let's find out if knowledge is infinite. To be infinite it should not be limited in space, time or object identity. It should be every-where, every-time and in everything."*

"*Regarding SPACE; Earlier we saw that knowledge exists in 'different places' like our thoughts, memories, imagination, experiences, books, magazines, radio, internet, television and so on. Knowledge is 'scattered everywhere' in different places. The knowledge in a Grammar book isn't the same as the knowledge in a Science book or Movie Magazine. The knowledge in my mind is different from the knowledge in your mind. There isn't any kind of knowledge that is the same everywhere. Knowledge is limited in space; it is NOT omnipresent."*

"Regarding TIME; Knowledge is definitely limited in time. A thought in your mind comes and goes, the knowledge in a book has a time of creation and will have a time of destruction, your dreams have a starting point and ending point in time, every experience has a starting point and ending point in time too. There isn't any knowledge that always was, is and will always be. Knowledge is limited in time; it is NOT eternal or timeless."

"And OBJECT IDENTITY; Knowledge is also most definitely limited in object identity. The knowledge of one object doesn't apply to another object. The knowledge of sound is different from the knowledge of smell, taste, sight, dreams etc. Different objects give different knowledge. The knowledge of one object is different from the knowledge of another object. Knowledge is limited by objects; knowledge is NOT non-dual."

David interrupted, *"I got it! KNOWLEDGE CANNOT BE INFINITE because what I know 'here' isn't true in another place, what I know 'now' I didn't know before and also what I 'know' is not the only thing I know! Knowledge FAILS the test of infinity."* Yogiji smiled and said, *"Very good my boy but the ancient scriptures written by enlightened sages can't be off the mark. There must be truth in them. Let us try and find if there is anything in knowledge that 'fits' the infinity definition."*

"We gain knowledge about things by perceiving or experiencing them. How do you 'know' that you have knowledge? There is something inside that says, "I'm aware that I know this and that." It's not the mind either because that something inside also knows that you have a mind which you experience all the time. For example, you know your feelings; you know that you have thoughts; you experience the mind feeling sad, happy, disturbed, stressed and so on."

"Your mind 'thinks' about something, and your intellect 'knows and understands' things but still something inside us is 'aware' that we know. For example, 6+3+11=? What is calculating the answer is the mind, when you get the answer (20) it's the intellect that knows 6+3+11=20 the answer, lastly the ego steps in and says, "I know the answer is 20." Yet there is something else inside you that can say 'I'm aware that I know the answer'. What is that something?"

"The intellect is 'perceived' or 'seen' by your CONSCIOUSNESS. Consciousness is 'aware' that the intellect knows. Consciousness 'watches and witnesses' everything in the mind and intellect without getting involved in any way. The thoughts in the mind and intellect arise and subside in your consciousness or in your awareness. You are conscious or aware of the thoughts in your mind and intellect yet your mind and intellect can't be aware or conscious of you!"

"Thus the 'witness' of all knowledge is Consciousness. Why are we calling Consciousness a 'witness'? It's because Consciousness is simply 'aware' of what the mind and intellect think. It doesn't actively participate in thinking or acquiring the knowledge. Consciousness remains in the background and 'watches or witnesses' the activity of your mind and intellect. Without Consciousness one cannot have any knowledge. The underlying constant reality of all knowledge is Consciousness. Now let's see if Consciousness can pass the infinity test we did earlier." Uchit remembered and quickly scribbled down something on another new page....

"Knowledge"
Is
Different In
Different Spaces,
Unknown, Known
And Forgotten
At different
Times &
Is of Numerous
Different Types!

Yogiji carried on, *"Regarding SPACE; you are not only conscious of everything that you can see or perceive, but all the things that you can't directly see or perceive, all exist in your consciousness. You may have never been to outer space to see the other planets in our galaxy, yet all the other planets exist in your consciousness or awareness in the form of knowledge."*

"Consciousness or awareness is not limited to any Space. Ask yourself this question, "Is the Universe in my Consciousness or is my Consciousness in the Universe?" You'll find that the entire Universe exists in your Consciousness. Consciousness is everywhere at the same time. CONSCIOUSNESS IS OMNIPRESENT!" Yogiji said enthusiastically.

"And regarding TIME; Consciousness has been present since you were born and will continue to be till your last breath. When the body dies, consciousness doesn't die, it simply ceases to exist in the body. Death of the body doesn't mean death of Consciousness. You have been 'experiencing' something or the other all the time since your birth."

"Your entire life is made up of experiences. As long as you are conscious, you are experiencing. Experience or knowledge of different objects at different times is 'witnessed' by the underlying reality of Consciousness. There is never a point in time that consciousness came into being and there never will be a point in time that consciousness will cease to be. Consciousness is ever unchanging and time exists in consciousness, consciousness doesn't exist in time. Therefore, we can conclude that Consciousness is not limited in time. CONSCIOUSNESS IS TIMELESS OR ETERNAL!"

"Finally regarding OBJECT IDENTITY; Consciousness is the one ever-unchanging underlying reality of all knowledge or experiences. Whether you read a book, watch a movie, think a thought, take a walk in the park, play a game with friends, the 'one' background Consciousness remains unchanged. Consciousness is not limited by different knowledge or experiences from different objects. It is the same ONE Consciousness that is aware of all knowledge and experiences. CONSCIOUSNESS IS NON-DUAL!" Yogiji completed looking quite satisfied with himself, *"David I would gladly invite you to challenge anything I have just said. Do you have any questions or doubts?"*

David looked at Yogiji and motioned his hand to give him a moment to take it all in. *"Hmmm, if my consciousness is everywhere, then why does it feel like it's just in my body and not on that other empty seat, on your seat, on the floor or in New York right now? Also if consciousness is eternal then what about when one is in deep sleep, in an almost unconsciousness state, where is consciousness then?" "Great questions David and I'm glad you asked them."*

"To answer your first question about Consciousness not being on the floor or in New York right now, try to see it this way. The other empty seat, my seat, the floor and New York are all in 'your' consciousness right now aren't they? You are conscious or aware of the space between your seat and the empty seat, you are conscious of New York right now otherwise you couldn't have mentioned any of these things or places. They all exist in 'your' consciousness."

"And to answer your second question about the unconscious state during deep sleep. When you wake up after a good sound sleep, you normally would say, "I slept like a log, I didn't know where I was" or something similar. Now 'who' reports the fact that you slept like a log? Something must have been aware that you slept like a log otherwise you would not 'know' you had slept for that much time. In deep sleep, you don't experience the body or the mind (dreams) but consciousness continues to 'witness' during deep sleep and upon waking up the mind reports an 'absence' of experiences."

"Deep sleep is not an absence of experience; it is an experience of absence. And so when you wake up, your consciousness is aware that you experienced 'no-thing' during that time, but you did experience the 'nothingness.'" I hope that clears out your doubts David. These are very common questions and I'm glad you asked them." David was so involved by now and paid attention to each word Yogiji was saying. This conversation had depth and substance in it and also he could not find any fault or loophole to prove Yogiji wrong in any way. Uchit looked at both Yogiji and David before declaring aloud, *"This is uchit!"* and wrote down the following on a new page.....

"Consciousness" Is Omnipresent, Timeless & Non-Dual!

The train had slowed down quite a bit and David looked at the time, it was almost 1pm which meant they had just a few minutes before they arrived at Dehradun Station. The last call for tea and coffee was doing the rounds in the train and all three grabbed a coffee, some strong caffeine was definitely required.

Yogiji looked at David, *"The last word 'Truth', I'll explain that on the onward journey from Dehradun. We'll take a taxi from here; it's a three-hour drive to Vatsalya Village and we'll stop over at Mussoorie for some afternoon tea. Swamiji has a very close friend who would like to meet you there. Let's have some lunch in Dehradun before embarking on the rest of the journey. Anyone hungry?"* asked Yogiji.

Uchit looked excited as the train came to a complete standstill, *"I know the best local restaurant in town, I lived in Dehradun for over three years and I know it like the back of my hand."*

They got off the train and Uchit led them to the local taxi stand where they hired an old Ambassador taxi for their onward journey to Vatsalya Village. Uchit negotiated with the driver and closed the deal at just two thousand rupees for the 180km journey. David was amazed at how cheap the travel was in India. When converted it was hardly thirty-five dollars for almost 200km. *"What a bargain!"* exclaimed David patting Uchit on the back.

The Ambassador is one of the oldest taxis available in India and undoubtedly gives the smoothest ride compared to any of the new model taxis. Once inside the cab, David and Yogiji took the backseat that was comparable to a two-seater sofa and Uchit jumped on the navigators seat next to the driver. After a short conversation between Uchit and the driver in the local language, the driver slowly pulled out of the taxi stand and they were on their way to the restaurant for lunch before heading towards Vatsalya Village.

David couldn't help but notice the scenery all round, Dehradun is a major tourist spot mainly because it is near the Himalayan foothills. Waterfalls, greenery all around, cool climate and the mountains on the sides of the meandering roads make the ride very scenic. David was relishing the view and taking in the fresh air.

They stopped at an open air hill view restaurant that had just a few wooden beds called *'manji'* that everyone sat on. Uchit didn't ask anyone what they wanted and ordered the most popular dish *'chole-puri'* for everyone, once they finished that, three tall glasses of *'kulfi-falooda'* were presented which all three again relished with utmost satisfaction.

As they got up to leave, the restaurant owner called for complimentary *'paan'* for them. Back on the road after a delicious lunch, they all took a short twenty minutes nap in the taxi while the driver sung along to the local songs playing on the radio. Mussorrie was about an hours drive away.

A swift swerve on one of the road bends woke up everyone and Yogiji sat upright. Everyone was wide-awake and alert. *"Switch off the radio."* Yogiji told the driver, which he did immediately. *"David, I have one last word to explain to you before we get to Mussorrie and meet up with Swamiji's friend."* David immediately splashed some water from his water bottle on his face to freshen up a little and Uchit pulled out the notebook from the bag. Both eager to hear what Yogiji had to say.

TRUTH

"Just checking, do you still remember the definition of Brahman?" asked Yogiji sounding like a teacher, *"Yes! Brahman is Truth, Knowledge, Infinity simultaneously,"* replied David and Uchit both in unison. *"Great! The word 'truth' comes from the word 'true'. For anything to be true it must be real, a fact, accurate and without variation. According to the ancient scriptures truth is that which is ever unchanging or is permanent. It must be true in every circumstance, situation, place, time and every object that we can perceive. According to the definition of Brahman, truth must be knowledge and infinite otherwise it won't fit the definition."*

"Let's look around us and try to identify what we think is real or true. This taxi is real, this bag is real, the mountains are real, the driver is real, this water bottle is real and in fact everything we see, hear, smell, touch, taste, think, remember or know, is real. Things and objects are as real as thoughts, memories and imagination. We are in the middle of an ocean of real objects and things." Uchit turned the page and scribbled with the marker on a new page…

Other Names
For
"Truth"
Are;
True, Real,
Reality, Fact,
'Accurate
Without Variation'.

"Good, now put any of these 'real' things to the 'knowledge' and 'infinity' test and let's determine if this is what the scriptures are talking about. Taking up knowledge first, all the things you just mentioned as real; the bottle, mountain, bag, taxi, driver and so on are all without a doubt, knowledge. This is a taxi – that's knowledge. These are mountains – that's knowledge. Everything you 'know' to be real IS knowledge! TRUTH IS KNOWLEDGE!"

"Let's check to see if truth passes the infinity test. Are all the 'real' objects we mentioned every-where, every-time and every-thing? It doesn't sound right, but still let's reason it out."

"Regarding SPACE; this bag is here and definitely not everywhere. It is occupying only a small amount of space in the taxi and not any other space. The same with the mountain, the bottle, the driver and in fact any object you can think of will be occupying a certain amount of space and not the entire Universe. If you can say that something is where it is and not everywhere, then it is limited in space. You'll soon find out that every-thing is limited in space. Things or objects are NOT omnipresent!"

"Regarding TIME; all objects are definitely limited in time. They all have a point in time when they came into being and there will come a point in time when they cease to exist as they are. This bag was created on a certain date, and will be destroyed sometime in the future. The mountain came into being after the volcano eruptions and has already changed in so many ways since it came into being. Your thoughts are also real things; they are also limited in time. Thoughts arise and subside. Every real thing you can think of will have a time of creation and a time of destruction, in between these two points in time it exists. Your shoes were created and will be destroyed in the future. You get the idea right? Every-thing is limited in time. Things or objects are NOT eternal!"

"And regarding OBJECT IDENTITY; this too is very easy to see right away. No object is every-thing. This taxi is not the bag or the mountain. Your shoes are not the shirt, this driver is not the water bottle and so on. You can see that every object is just that particular object and not everything in the Universe. Every object or thing is limited to being itself and not any thing else in the Universe. Every-thing or object (real, true, truth) is definitely limited in Object Identity. Things or objects are NOT non-dual!"

"What we consider to be 'real' or 'true' FAILS the infinity test. So, just like we did with 'knowledge', let's look deeper into 'truth' and see if we can uncover any 'underlying' reality. Something that is every-where, every-time and in every-thing." "That would be a miraculous discovery!" said David nudging an elbow on Uchit who quickly opened a new page and wrote the following...

> Everything We Consider To Be "Real" or "True" Is Limited In Space, Time & Object Identity.

"Let's take a look," said Yogiji with a smile. *"You said the bag is real, the taxi is real, the mountain is real, the water bottle is real and so on. The scriptures point out something that we all take for granted and show us what actually is real in all the things you just pointed out. The bag IS, the taxi IS, the mountain IS, the driver IS, the water bottle IS, David IS.*

IS, IS, IS, everything 'IS'. The word 'IS' tells us that the object or thing EXISTS. Think about it. Everything we can perceive has to 'exist' before it can be a thing or object. "It must have EXISTENCE before anything else!"

"EXISTENCE is the 'underlying reality' of anything that we can perceive. Take the water bottle again and put it though the test. Every atom of the bottle exists, that's why the bottle is there in the first place. Before it was made into a bottle, the plastic existed, maybe as a lump of plastic. The notebook existed as a tree before being cut into wood and being rolled into paper. After the creation, the notebook exists now and if we were to tear it right now, it will still "exist" as torn pieces of paper, if we break that down further, whatever results will still have existence in it."

"Suppose we burn the notebook. The burnt ashes exist! We can break down anything to its smallest particles, molecules and atoms but existence always remains, even though the form, shape, size and so on may change. 'Existence' is the ever-unchanging underlying reality of the ocean of things we consider real or true." Uchit noted that quickly on another new page...

"Existence" Is The Ever-Unchanging, Underlying Reality In Everything That We Can Perceive!

"Now the question arises "Is Existence 'infinite' in space, time and object identity?

Regarding SPACE; Existence is not limited in space. Space is everywhere. There is no place in the entire Universe where Space is not! The words 'here', 'there', 'where', 'somewhere', 'everywhere', 'place', all denote that 'space' is present. Space has to 'exist' before we can call it space. Every-where = Every-space! So we can say that, EXISTENCE IS OMNIPRESENT!"

"Regarding TIME; "Is Existence eternal or timeless?" If we can think of a time that 'didn't' exist, then it would make sense to ask this question. Time also exists! Time has to exist before we can call it time. The words 'time, before, after, during, again' all denote existence of time in the past, present or future. Every-time = Every-existence! Thus, we can confirm that, EXISTENCE IS ETERNAL OR TIMELESS!"

"And regarding OBJECT IDENTITY; we are in the middle of an ocean of existence, there is only one existence and it is in everything we can perceive. The objects may vary in size, shape, and form. They vary in the spaces that they occupy and they definitely vary from each other BUT the underlying reality in all of them is the same one constant unchanging 'existence'. In fact it would not be wrong to say that we see 'existence' in the form of this bag, mountain, taxi, marker, bottle and so on. There is no-thing that is 'apart' from existence. We can confirm EXISTENCE IS NON-DUAL!" One look at Uchit from David and he scribbled the following on a new page...

"Existence" Is Omnipresent, Timeless & Non-Dual!

"Thus, we have uncovered the underlying meanings of the definition 'Brahman is Truth, Knowledge, Infinity simultaneously.' And we can now safely say 'Brahman is Infinite Existence & Infinite Consciousness Simultaneously.'

David questioned, *"So what you're trying to say is that the Supreme Being (Brahman) is Infinite Existence-Consciousness right?"* Yogiji replied, *"Yes my son! The Supreme Being, Brahman is 'pure' existence and 'pure' consciousness simultaneously. Pure Existence and Pure Consciousness are both 'formless and infinite' and together they're called Brahman that pervades the entire Universe."*

Yogiji continued, *"Just like I said, the Supreme Being (Brahman) is Every-where, Every-time & Every-thing."* David replied, *"That's fine but I still don't see Brahman. All I still see are the taxi, mountains, bag, marker and numerous objects all apart from each other. Why can't I see pure existence or perceive pure consciousness? Are these two separate qualities of Brahman?"* asked David. Yogiji replied, *"They can't exist separately. Existence is 'known' and Consciousness 'exists'!"* Uchit was quick at noting this...

"Brahman"
The Supreme Being
Is
Pure Existence &
Pure Consciousness
Simultaneously.

"Existence Is Known
&
Consciousness Exists!

GURUJI IN MUSSORRIE

The driver took a final turn off the main road that led through a majestic gate towards an old white bungalow. They had arrived at Swamiji's friend's place. Mussoorie is at an altitude of almost five thousand feet and the road was all uphill and winding around the hills. No one had noticed anything along the way, as everyone except the driver was so engrossed in Yogiji's talk. They got off the car and Yogiji took them to the back of the bungalow from where they could see the entire city of Mussoorie also known as *'Queen of the Hills.'*

The bungalow was undeniably an ancient British structure from the colonial times and was built on the edge of a hill covered with trees and greenery. The weather was chilly and it felt like they were walking on clouds. A small wooden platform was built right over the edge and it was nothing short of a tourist spot that revealed the entire city before them. The market place had shops built along the main road that connected the city to the rest of the world. They could see the Himalayan snow ranges on one side and deep valleys covered with fog on the other.

A young man of around eighteen years, wearing a white uniform came out from the bungalow's back door, walked towards them and greeted Yogiji by touching his feet and then hugging him. *"Master has been looking forward to your arrival since morning. He is seated in the main living area waiting for you all. Please follow me,"* said the young man. They followed the man into the bungalow and into the living area where beautiful antique wooden sofas and chairs with large pillows surrounded a large square wooden coffee table.

Large colorful hand paintings of people who looked like spiritual masters decorated the tall walls of the room. Seated on one of the royal looking chairs was an old man and Yogiji hurried towards him, touching his feet, *"Guruji, how have you been? It's so nice to see you again. Swamiji sends his regards and says he will visit you as soon as the weather gets a little warmer. Everything looks the same since my last visit almost six months ago,"* said Yogiji looking around the living area.

The old man signaled us to have a seat. *"Guruji, this is David from America and we're on our way to the ashram where Swamiji has permitted him to stay for a few days with us. Swamiji has requested you to share some of your wisdom with David before he meets him. You know Swamiji trusts you the most with the visitors he gets from the west."* David looked surprised but decided to speak out expressing what he had come for. *"Can I call you Guruji too?"* asked David looking at the old man, *"Yes you may,"* came Gurujis answer in a deep strong British accent that left David pleasantly surprised.

"Thank you Guruji. I'm in search of someone who has seen God and can show me God, and that's what has brought me to India. I'm really hoping Swamiji can show me God like some of his disciples who claim he did it for them. Since my arrival this morning Yogiji has been discussing 'Brahman' with me and I sort of get it but I'm still not completely convinced about it. Maybe you can shed some more light on it?" Guruji sat up straight, called one of the houseboys and asked him to prepare tea and some snacks for everyone.

"My boy, come and sit in front of me so we can look directly at each other while talking." David obliged and sat on a stool before Guruji. Being so close he could not help but feel warmth and love that he had never experienced before. He had heard that being in the presence of an enlightened master one would feel undeniable grace and a continuous stream of unconditional love and warmth. This is exactly how he was feeling now.

There was a certain mystic glow on Guruji's face as he made strong eye contact with David. He looked like the perfect great grandfather. Long white beard, round black reading glasses, small in stature and looked at everyone with warm loving eyes. You could tell that he rarely ever got angry. Just being in his presence made everyone around him peaceful. David understood why Swamiji asked to see him before coming to the ashram. Guruji's command over the English language made him the perfect person to share wisdom with foreigners. David was already feeling the love and warmth of the hospitality being offered.

Looking directly into David's eyes Guruji spoke in a deep velvety voice, *"Brahman is formless and infinite and anything that is formless or infinite can't be seen directly (perceived) unless it takes a form. What we see through our sense of sight (eyes) is only innumerable visual forms. All objects that are in our vision are simply different 'forms' with different 'names' of the same 'one infinite existence.'"*

"To recognize existence it needs a form. Every thing or object that we perceive has a form."
"What our ancient Scriptures tell us is to recognize the 'existence' in everything that we see with our eyes and not just relate to the name and form of the object."

David asked, *"Guruji, Consciousness is also formless and infinite according to what I have understood from Yogiji. The formless can't be perceived in any way, which means that we can't 'directly know or experience' pure consciousness. So does Consciousness also need something to be able to recognize it?"*

"That's a good question David. Yes, you can't directly 'know' or 'experience' Consciousness. Remember, to appreciate or recognize the formless it needs a form. You can only recognize consciousness when it perceives or experiences a form as well. This includes everything in the Universe. Our eyes only see numerous 'forms' but what about all the other forms that are not visible to the eyes such as sound, touch, smell, taste, feelings, thoughts, imagination, memories, emotions, knowledge and so on? All these are 'different forms' of existence that aren't visible to the sense of sight (eyes). Yet we perceive all of them and we know they exist. We experience all these other kinds of forms as well."

"To recognize Consciousness you simply need any kind of knowledge or any object present in your awareness. The very fact that you 'know' or 'experience' anything means you are conscious. I know this is a bag – is knowledge, I hear the birds in the fores,t is knowledge, your name is David, is knowledge, we are in Mussoorie, is knowledge and so on. The fact that I know anything means I am conscious or aware of it. There can be no knowledge or experience outside consciousness. You cannot know or experience anything without being conscious or aware first."

"Pure Existence and Pure Consciousness are the 'only' two formless underlying realities that are Omnipresent, Eternal and Non-Dual and pervade the entire Universe together as one. Both existence and consciousness are infinite, that is, they are not limited in space, time or object identity."

"Just like fire and heat, sun and sunlight, flowers and fragrance are intrinsic to one another, the basic nature of fire is heat, the nature of the Sun is light and the nature of flowers is fragrance in the same way Existence and Consciousness are also intrinsic to one another, that is, they cannot exist independent of each other. 'Brahman' is the name given to this 'infinite intrinsic combination' of existence and consciousness."

"Everything that 'exists' is Brahman. Everything that you 'know' is Brahman. There is no other entity 'apart' from Brahman. Therefore Brahman pervades the entire Universe. Brahman is the One Supreme Universal Being, the Absolute Reality."

"How do you know you have eyes?" asked Guruji, *"Because I can see"* replied David. *"What do you need to see to be very sure that you have eyes?"* asked Guruji immediately, *"I can look at the reflection of my eyes in the mirror,"* said David. *"That's not a very clever answer my boy, you need not see a reflection of your eyes to be sure you have eyes. They very fact that you can 'see' confirms that you have eyes. And see what? See anything at all!"*

"In the same way all objects (physical and non-physical) are perceived only through their different forms. They all 'exist' and you are 'conscious' of that fact! Look around anywhere, anytime and recognize the "One Existence in everything you perceive & One Consciousness that perceives everything!"

The Absolute Reality = Brahman,
Brahman = Infinite Existence + Infinite Consciousness.

"If you can recognize and abide as "Pure Consciousness" that is also conscious of your body, mind and intellect, and erase all names and forms from everything you see or perceive, then you are seeing or perceiving Brahman - the Absolute Reality as He/She/It should be seen or perceived, that is, EVERY-WHERE, EVERY-TIME and in EVERY-THING with OPEN EYES!" David looked at Uchit and he understood at once. He pulled out the notebook and on a new page he wrote down....

> "Recognize The ONE Unbroken Existence In Everything & The ONE Unbroken Consciousness That Perceives Everything."

"My son I know what you're thinking. You're looking at all the things around here and thinking to yourself, 'I can't see pure existence, all I see right here and now are chairs, tables, cushions, a roof, walls, windows, a rug on the floor and so on. How am I to see Brahman? Well, it's the knowledge that's important as well. If I asked you what color is the sky?" "Blue!" exclaimed Uchit with a big grin on his face. Guruji looked at David, *"The sky is colorless Guruji, I've learned that in high school."* "That's uchit David!" said Guruji who had picked up on the name game as well.

"You know the sky is colorless, yet when you look at the sky in the daytime it still 'appears' to be blue. In the same way an oasis of water in the desert when seen from a closer distance reveals itself to be a mirage. Once you know it's a mirage when you walk away from the spot and look back, what do you see? The same oasis of water appears again from the distance, but now you have the knowledge that the water is only an appearance, it's not real. The face that you see in the mirror is not your real actual face. The face on your head is the reality, not the reflected face. The face in the mirror only appears there, it's not really there."

"In the same way, look at this chair, table, rug, walls, windows and 'know' them to be existence. They appear as things and objects with a name and form but their reality is 'existence'. Everything in the Universe will appear exactly as you have seen them before but now you 'know' their reality is 'existence'."

"Brahman – the Absolute Reality is in every experience and every object, being veiled by just a name and form. All we see or perceive are 'names and forms' and not the underlying formless existence and consciousness. In simpler words 'names and forms' veil or hide Brahman before our very eyes. If you erase the names and forms you perceive Brahman. It's as simple as that or as difficult as that my boy! The sky will not cease appearing to be blue because you know it is colorless. The water of the mirage won't cease to appear because you know it's a mirage."

"Seeing Existence As Consciousness or Being Conscious of Existence Is Brahman – the Absolute Reality!" Guruji was on fire as he spoke with such passion that everyone was hypnotized by his words. Uchit scribbled again quickly on a new page...

Brahman Is Veiled By Names & Forms & Thoughts.

Erase Them And You Are Experiencing God/Brahman.

"My son, now you can ask these questions. Where is Brahman? The answer - Where is it not? When is Brahman? The answer - When is it not? Which object is Brahman? The answer - "Which object is it not?" The Absolute reality -Brahman is EVERY-WHERE, EVERY-TIME & EVERY-THING! You just need to start recognizing it!" said Guruji turning his head towards the houseboy who had just walked in with a large tray containing cups, saucers, a variety of delicious looking snacks and a large kettle with steam coming out its spout.

He placed the tray on the coffee table and handed out plates to everyone and served the snacks that included *farsan, chevda, potato crisps* and a variety of Indian sweets of which David recognized the *laddoos, gulab jamun and chocolate barfi.* Uchit couldn't resist the sweet aromas but one look from David and he scratched his head trying to remember what Guruji had just said. Quickly he noted down on a new page before taking his first spoonful of *chevda...*

The Absolute Reality "Brahman" Is Every-where, Every-time, Every-thing!

Start Recognizing That Absolute Reality Everyday In Everything You See And Do!

"My son, is there any doubt in your mind about Brahman – The Absolute Reality? How, when and where to see or perceive Brahman? Also whether you doubt about it being the Absolute Reality or the Supreme Being?" asked Guruji. David looked at Guruji, gathered some courage and said, *"Guruji, I get what Yogiji had explained to me before we got here, and you have made it completely clear to me. I understand Brahman to the extent that you both have explained to me. Brahman is the One Absolute Reality, it is the One Supreme Being and its definition is Existence, Consciousness and Infinity. Both Pure Existence and Pure Consciousness are 'formless' and 'infinite'. We perceive pure existence and pure consciousness only through names and forms."*

"Therefore the reality of everything in the Universe is Brahman. In fact it is only Brahman "appearing" as every-thing in the Universe. So everything I can see or perceive externally or internally, with my senses or my mind has a name and form BUT the ONE underlying reality in everything is Brahman (Infinite Existence and Consciousness simultaneously). I can now recognize Brahman everywhere, every time and in everything. This is a remarkable observation and can't be denied by any philosopher, scientist, religion or any common man with a sane mind because you have not asked me to believe in anything blindly. Everything you have explained is right here and now."

"But Guruji, my question is still unanswered and I have one more added to the original question now. You have shown me the Absolute Reality here and now, but where is God in all this? And another question that now pops up after understanding all this is, who or where am I, You and every other living being in all this? I hope it's a valid question Guruji?" asked David.

Guruji looked at David with smile and he nodded his head with a sparkle in his eyes. *"My son, I am impressed with your grasping skills. Your burning desire to meet God is evident. You have also understood Brahman – the Absolute Reality with great clarity 'so far'. And your questions are absolutely valid at this point; in fact I am delighted that you asked them because if you have understood that the entire Universe appears in the 'One Supreme Being' referred to as 'Brahman', then where do 'you' stand in all this? Are you, me, Yogiji and everyone else, apart from Brahman? Are we all Brahman? If so, why don't you feel it? Why aren't you omnipresent or eternal? Such questions should arise and I am so glad you brought them up. There is one final point you need to know, understand and REALIZE for yourself about Brahman that will not only solve but dissolve all your questions and for that Swamiji is the best person. I believe you are headed to Vatsalya Village to meet him. You are indeed a blessed soul. Very few people get the opportunity to meet Swamiji one-on-one in person."*

"The final part of Brahman, that Swamiji will himself tell you about has to not only be heard and understood BUT EXPERIENCED AND REALIZED by yourself. After that you will have no questions whatsoever about anything in the Universe to ask anyone. This is the knowledge, understanding, experience and realization of all the great saints and sages who have walked the earth. When you manage to do it yourself, there will be no difference between you and any of the great saints who see and talk to God all the time. I think my work and Yogiji's work here is done. You may still clear any more doubts that arise on the way to Vatsalya Village, I'm sure Yogiji would be glad to clear them. Alternatively you may give your mind a break, ponder over what you have understood and look out the car window, as the scenery along the way is incredibly beautiful during winter. Give my regards to Swamiji and ask him to visit us soon," said Guruji.

MUSSORRIE TO VATSALYA

All three took leave from Guruji and were on their way to Vatsalya Village, it was exactly twenty minutes past three o'clock in the afternoon and the wind blowing into the car was cool and refreshing. All three sat quietly soaking in the scenery along the road as the driver sang along with the old songs playing on the radio. David was smiling at what he had learnt so far but couldn't wait to meet Swamiji. Secretly smiling to himself and letting the wind hit his face from the window, it was already a great start to his indefinite vacation he had taken from the busy city life in New York City.

The supposedly two-hour drive seemed to pass by very quickly. David admired the hills, the waterfalls, they had stopped on the way to change a punctured tire and they saw squirrels, exotic birds chirping and villagers carrying water pots along the way. It was surely a memorable scenic drive. David contemplated on what Guruji had said; he started to look at everything as *existence* in one form or another. He had understood the point both Yogiji and Guruji had made about things *existing* before their form was perceived and a name given to them.

He looked out the car window and thought to himself, *"There's existence in the form of trees, existence in the form of grass and the hills, existence in the form of birds flying high up in the sky, existence as the sky and clouds, existence in the form of the car they were seated in. How unbelievably amazing, artistic and creative. The same ONE existence playing in so many different forms all together at the same time had to be a wonder in itself."*

Uchit, seated in the front seat looked back and saw David smiling to himself and couldn't hesitate to ask him, *"Sir, why are you smiling?"* David with an even wider smile on his face said, *"You know we always look at things in the world as they are, for example, see those birds flying in the air, they look beautiful, see those cows on the hill grazing, look at the other cars on the road going past us, in fact see everything going on around us at this very moment."*

"We look at a particular thing or object and either like what we see or don't like what we see, a lot of things are not even noticed in the background of what we focus on, such as, we didn't notice the bushes when we looked at the cows grazing." Things are usually good, bad or ugly. This is how we all see the world around us. Specific things happening around us that we give our attention to. But after the talk with Guruji I can't but help admiring and falling in love with this Brahman." "And why is that?" asked Yogiji who was almost dozing off but sat upright wide awake, rather startled by what he'd just heard.

"Yogiji, all the things in the world, rather in the Universe should I say, every little thing that is happening right now like somewhere a child has just taken birth, somewhere a lion has just pounced on a deer, clouds are moving, the wind is blowing, rivers are flowing, flowers are blooming and all the terrible things as well like someone may have just gotten a heart attack, someone is battling for their life in a hospital, a lover just dumped their partner, someone just got their dream job, another has just lost his dream job."

"Just to realize that everything happening in the entire Universe at any one given moment is happening on ONE CANVAS OF EXISTENCE."

"ONE Existence is playing all these roles at the same time all over the Universe simultaneously! Absolutely mind boggling to say the least," said David staring outside the window lost in his thoughts. Yogiji looked amazed, he had never thought of Brahman in this way. He gently patted David on his back with a smile on his face as they finally drove into Vatsalya Village at exactly twelve minutes past six o'clock in the evening.

The red-orange Sun setting behind the hills was a truly beautiful and breath taking sight. The ashram was at the top of one of the hills with a small road leading to its entrance. The gate keepers opened the gate after recognizing Yogiji in the back seat, the driver drove into a long lane with trees on both sides that led up to a parking area where only one four wheel drive open Jeep with muddy wheels was parked.

They all got off the car. The driver requested to stay the night because it gets dark very early and its not safe to drive at night. He was also tired and immediately one of the staff from the main house escorted him to a driver's quarter where he would be fed and given a place to stay the night. David and Uchit stretched out their arms and legs looking around the ashram. As they followed Yogiji towards the dimly lit main house they saw nicely kept lawns with trees at the edge, flowers filled the air with mixed fragrances and birds sang at the treetops.

They walked into the building that looked like a reception area for visitors. The almost eleven hour long journey had come to an end. They were in Vatsalya Village at the ashram just before sunset. David felt he had already lived a lifetime in just the journey to get here. Back in New York City, everyday, was the same mechanical grind all happening within just a couple of miles radius within the city. This journey to get to Vatsalya Village on its own was a lifetime's experience.

Yogiji excused himself and headed towards a different part of the ashram. As David looked around the reception area, he saw a large framed picture of Swamiji with some devotees and just below the huge frame was an image of a finger pointing right at David with the saying, *"Aham Brahma Asmi."* David asked the young monk behind the reception counter, *"Hey dude, what does that saying under Swamiji's picture mean?"* pointing towards the framed photo.

"Sir, Aham Brahma Asmi means I am Brahman," replied the innocent looking monk. David was taken aback, *"WHAT???? HE IS BRAHMAN??? YOU MEAN SWAMIJI IS BRAHMAN? HE IS THE ABSOLUTE REALITY?"* exclaimed David, *"HOW???? WHAT DOES THIS MEAN??? SURELY THIS IS NOT POSSIBLE! HOW CAN HE BE BRAHMAN???"*

The young monk sensed he had said too much, *"Sir, please sign this check-in form. These are the keys to your room, please freshen up and Swamiji will meet you at 7pm sharp in the dining hall for dinner."* David stood still, shocked at what he had just heard. *"Swamiji thinks he is God? That's Impossible! Have I wasted my time and money to come this far to meet a fraudster?"* thought David to himself.

With mixed emotions he picked up the keys and followed the young monk leading them to their room. *"I have to meet this guy and give him a piece of my mind. Everyone warned me about fake gurus in India and look what I found? Someone who thinks he is God! Aaargh!"* David couldn't wait to meet Swamiji now.

"Aham Brahma Asmi"

AFTER THE STORY

This is the end of part one of the series "I Am Consciousness". With logical reasoning that no one can deny scientifically, philosophically, religiously or spiritually, Yogiji explains to David the definition of Brahman which is infinite pure existence and infinite pure consciousness. No one can deny that everything that they know, first *exists* in some *form* or another and then only its given a name. The flat piece of wood with four legs has to *exist* before we can call it a wooden table.

This applies not only to all physical and tangible things but to all subtle, intangible and invisible things too such as emotions, memories, thoughts, feelings etc All our life is one continuous experience from birth to death. To know or experience anything we *must* be conscious. We know and experience millions of things during our lifetime but they're all known or experienced in the one backdrop called Consciousness. If you learn to separate consciousness from the mind, you will become aware of the thoughts coming into your mind.

Just as you are aware of the different sounds coming in through your ears, different colors coming in through your eyes, different tastes coming in through your tongue, different smells coming in through your nose and different sensations coming in through your skin, in the same way, you will become aware of the different thoughts coming into your mind.

Try this simple exercise; think a thought then pause for 4-5 seconds and then think another different thought. For example mentally think 2+2=4, pause for 5 seconds, now think 4+4=8. Mentally *see* the two thoughts and become aware of them and also become aware of the pause between the two thoughts. What you are required to do is become 'aware' or be 'conscious' of the two thoughts *separated* by a pause in which there was no thought. During this pause there was only pure awareness, you were aware of things around you but there was no thought in the mind which means that you are aware or conscious of your thoughts. You could also say that all your thoughts arise and subside in your awareness or your consciousness.

This is a remarkable discovery for those who think that they are nothing more beyond the body and mind (both your body and mind are objects that are experienced in your consciousness or awareness). It is even more astonishing for those who think that the mind is a sentient or conscious entity, it is not! (You are conscious of your mind, your mind isn't conscious of you.)

Everything in the entire Universe is experienced through only five senses in the form of smell, sound, sight, touch and taste. All the five senses are experienced by the one mind in the form of different thoughts. Millions of thoughts in the mind all arise and subside in the one pure unchanging awareness or consciousness.

With this logical explanation and reasoning the Upanishad shows us practically that the Supreme Being, known as Brahman (you can call it by any name) is all around us everywhere, all the time and in everything. This is the first part of understanding what Brahman – The Absolute Reality is. You, the reader, should logically be able to *'see or perceive'* Brahman in all your normal daily activities by the end of this part.

In the 2nd part of this series, titled "I Am Brahman", which is a continuation of the same story, David meets Swamiii at the ashram in Vatsalya Village. Swamiji explains and answers all David's questions and clears his doubts about where *'you'* as an individual are in this infinite Brahman.

Shocking at first but with clear logic and reasoning presented by the same Upanishad one realizes that, *"I am Brahman, I am the Absolute Reality"*. One begins to understand what all the Saints and Sages in the past actually meant in their wise sayings and writings such as, *'There is but one God", "We are all one", "You are the entire Universe", "You are not a drop in the ocean, you are the entire ocean in a drop,"* and many other such common wise sayings that you may have already come across.

One will also realize why an enlightened person behaves the way he or she does. Many pleasant surprises are experienced by David in the village. Swamiji gives detailed explanations of how there is only one reality which is our true nature with the help of interesting practical examples.

We look forward to you joining us on this incredible journey through the series which has been purposely broken down into small chunks that are easy to read.

EXTRA NOTES

The Vedas are the oldest Holy Scriptures known to mankind. The highest philosophical teachings in the Vedas are called the Upanishads. There are over 108 different Upanishads available that contain these teachings. The Upanishads are collectively known as Vedanta. Vedanta is made up of two words,. 'Veda' which means knowledge and 'anta' which means the end or the highest. Therefore Vedanta means 'the highest knowledge'. They contain the highest philosophical teachings of the Vedas.

Brahman is the Absolute Reality that is written about in all the Upanishads which tell us again and again that we are all that One Supreme Being and only if we could realize who or what we really are, then we would realize that we are in fact immortal, eternal, all pervading, infinite and pure bliss.

Such a realization would mean the end of any kind of fear including death, the end of all pain and suffering, the realization that we are the Universe or that the Universe appears within that Supreme Being which is your true reality.

It is the same realization that all the great saints and sages of all time had. They all realized the same one Universal Truth and spoke about it in different ways using different examples but ultimately they all point to the same one Universal Truth.

The path to Self-Realization and God-Realization is not an easy one. It requires enormous courage, persistence, patience, will-power, correct guidance (by an enlightened spiritual master who is well versed with the revealed scriptures himself, someone who not only knows what the scriptures are pointing to but is living and experiencing what the scriptures say. Just a note to add here, the Holy Scriptures of every religion point to the same Truth, so an enlightened spiritual master is necessary regardless of what religion they may belong to. The enlightened saint will never talk or preach about a certain religion, they will only point you to the One Universal Formless God and the utmost importance of realizing what our true nature is).

Ninety-nine percent of us are actually mediocre spiritual seekers and in fact most of us believe in God so that He can *better* our lives. We pray for worldly material things, we offer sacrifices or charity in return for something which may be material things or even our own happiness. *"I donate to charity because it makes me feel good to share with the less fortunate."* Do you see the selfishness in that? Now, don't misunderstand that to mean that it is not good to give to charity, the *intention* with which an act is performed makes all the difference. There is a saying that goes, *"The world will judge us based on our actions, but God will judge us based on our intentions."*

When seeking God or our true Self we cannot deceive the Supreme Being in any way including our thoughts, speech and actions. He is present within each one of us and has given us Human-beings the key to the doorway to becoming one with Him. You may ask why only human beings? In this world everything can be classified into two categories, living things and non-living things. Living things are further divided into two categories, the Plant Kingdom and the Animal Kingdom. Human beings fall into the animal kingdom and there is only one major difference which allows humans to be at the top of the animal kingdom and the entire existence. That one key is called 'intellect' and no other species apart from humans possess an intellect.

This intellect faculty of the mind allows us to reason, understand, plan ahead, research, develop, experiment and predict outcomes based on our understanding, reasoning and logic. This one difference allows humans to rule the planet. All other living things respond to their surroundings and react according to their instincts or stimuli.

The *intellect* is the key to Self-Realization and God-Realization. We have to understand and fully be convinced of what we want to achieve in this world. Here are a few *cliché* saying that relate to what's being said here: *"You are what you think." "The one who thinks he can and the one who thinks he can't are both usually right." "Think and grow rich." "Change your thoughts, change your life,"* and so on. All these sayings which you have come across many times are saying the same thing, whatever your goal in life, the intellect is the key to that doorway.

So, if you want to be an actor, you have to feed your mind and intellect with those particular thoughts and practices. If you want to become a sportsman, you have to feed your mind and intellect with those thoughts and practices. In the same way if you want to attain spiritual enlightenment you have to feed your mind and intellect with those particular thoughts and practices.

A great actor is one who loses himself in the character. A great singer is one who loses himself in the song. A great dancer is one who loses himself in the dance. A great artist is one who loses himself in the art. In the same way a great spiritual seeker is one who loses himself in the One he or she is seeking. These may not be easy words to understand at first but it is the final realization of every person who has achieved perfection in what they do.

If you can perceive an actor in the character portrayed on screen, if you can perceive an artist apart from the painting on the canvas, if you can perceive a singer apart from the song on the radio then there is something that has been held back by the actor, singer or painter. A great actor *'becomes'* the character, a great singer *'becomes'* the song, a great painter *'becomes'* the painting, a great dancer *'becomes'* the dance and a great seeker loses himself and becomes one with the God he or she is seeking.

Most people take this kind of statements and misinterpret them to mean that they or you will become "God" in this very limited and fragile body and mind complex. That is not what is being said. When you sincerely seek God, the seeker will eventually disappear, vanish or merge with God and all that will be left will be God. There will be no 'you' left as you earlier knew yourself to be.

In acting there is no actor, there's only a character, in singing there is no singer, there's only a song, in art there is no artist, there's only a master-piece, in dancing there is no dancer, there's only dance, in meditation there is no meditator, there's only the meditated, in devotion there is no devotee, there's only the beloved and in seeking there is no seeker, there's only the sought.

When you set out to seek God or the Self, don't be mediocre in your pursuit, give it all you have without holding back anything including yourself as you think you are. There are three steps in Vedanta to realizing your true nature.

The first step is to read or listen to the truths or the pointing's that the Spiritual master or scriptures are revealing. This means you should be able to repeat back the essence of what was said or written. At the end of this step you should be able to confirm that, *"I know what the enlightened master or scripture is saying but I don't understand it as yet!"*

The second step is to clear your doubts about what was said or written by reasoning, discussing, questioning and eliminating every possible obstacle that may give you even the slightest doubt that what is said or written may not be true. Do this until you are absolutely clear and understand WITHOUT A DOUBT that what is said or written is actually the truth. At the end of this step you should be able to confirm that, *"I know what you're saying and now I understand it!"*

The third step is to meditate or *'marinate'* yourself in that understanding everywhere, every time and in everything you do *until* it becomes a living reality for you. At the end of this step you will be saying, *"I know what you said, I not only understand it now but I AM IT!"*

ABOUT THE AUTHOR

Sukhdev Virdee was born and brought up in Nairobi, Kenya. Since childhood he was very inclined towards spirituality and music. After his studies he chose to take up music as a profession. He learnt how to play the keyboards and started performing live on stage at the age of nineteen. He later went to London and completed a BTEC in Music Production and Performance.

He later flew to Mumbai, India to pursue his dream of singing and composing music in the largest Indian Entertainment Industry. His debut pop-album became a chartbuster making him a popular household name in India and across the world. Mumbai became his home where he is known for his high energy live performances and this popularity took him to several countries across every continent on the planet to perform live for huge audiences.

A few more albums and singles followed after that. He was living the life that every young person looks up to even today. He had created a name for himself and enjoyed the name, fame and fortune that most singers dream of but never get to live. During all this he was totally oblivious of what life had in store for him in the coming years. Just before his 40th birthday, when he was going through a rather rough patch in life, three of his friends gifted him the Bhagavad Gita out of the blue. These were friends that he met only occasionally and yet within two weeks three different people gifted him the Bhagavad Gita which would change his life completely. He read the Bhagavad Gita and felt Lord Krishna was speaking directly to him. It completely changed his outlook towards life as he followed the teachings in the Bhagavad Gita as best as he could.

Just over a year later, one fine morning after he woke up from his morning meditation and walked towards his temple in the house, his body completely froze and in an instant he had become one with the entire Universe. Time stood still and every particle of the entire Universe was alive and shining in bright golden light and he was the light. He was no longer limited to just his body or mind, he was everywhere at the same time and everything was one with him.

This Spiritual awakening experience turned his life upside down and inside out. All desires for anything worldly vanished, fear of death vanished, love and compassion for entire humanity and nature arose and he could feel and experience the Supreme Being in everything.

Not knowing exactly what had happened and what to do next, he sought out several resources before he was pointed towards the Upanishads which answered all his questions as to what had happened, what led to it and what to do after such an awakening.

After years of studying the Vedanta texts he is now an expert on non-dual Vedanta through not only intellectual and philosophical knowledge but most importantly combined with his own personal daily experience.

He has put all his heart and soul into writing the *"I Am Consciousness"* book series that include the highest knowledge of the Upanishads and his own direct experience and knowledge of the Supreme Being.

The series has been written with absolute conviction that you, the reader, can realize your true immortal Universal Self too, that you are pure bliss and completely unaffected by all pain and suffering.

The promise of all spirituality is that one transcends pain and sorrow in this world, not that pain and sorrow don't come, but that the realized being is untouched by it. One realizes that their true nature is immortal, that they are one with the Universe. Would a being who realizes that he or she is one with the Universe ever want to accumulate anything in this world?

No, the True Saint or Sage who is Self-Realized makes do with only the very basic necessities required to live an honest decent life. They don't look to gain wealth, become famous, build an empire or any such sort of selfish activities.

Their main focus becomes serving humanity selflessly and uplifting others to help them realize their true nature so that they too can transcend suffering and realize their Oneness with the Universe. Sukhdev aims to do just that through his music, art and writing in the remaining days that he has left in this mortal body.

"I Am Consciousness"
6 Book Series
A Journey From Seeker
To Enlightened Master
Available As
E-books & Paperbacks
On Amazon & Other Digital Stores

Available As
E-books & Paperbacks
On Amazon & Other Digital Stores

VEDANTA EXAMPLES SIMPLIFIED

NON-DUALITY

SUKHDEV VIRDEE

THE DAY I MET GURU NANAK

NON-DUALITY

SUKHDEV VIRDEE

THE POWER OF NOTHING

NON DUALITY

SUKHDEV VIRDEE

A DIALOGUE WITH THE GOD OF DEATH

AS DEFINED BY THE UPANISHADS

SUKHDEV VIRDEE